the Wolf

Francesco Cesoni
Giovanni Fasoli

Translated by JMS Books

METRO BOOKS
NEW YORK

Contents

Wolves and humans

IT IS OBVIOUS THAT HUMANS HAVE BECOME THE DOMINANT BEINGS ON THIS PLANET. Only natural forces can restrain our arrogance and lack of respect for the environment – two things that distinguish us from other animal species. Nevertheless, we are also part of Earth's ecosystem; we too are bound by general rules whose subtlety and complexity we ignore. We think we can understand nature by simplifying and organizing it, but everything we do to it – from plundering its resources to oil spills, or even the simplest egg-thefts – has a cascade of repercussions on the fragile balance of the ecosystem.

The abstract, imaginary concept of the bloodthirsty wolf developed in this context of man's careless domination of nature. In fact, man and wolf have been in opposition since time immemorial. Their love-hate relationship began with the search for food. In prehistoric times, men and wolves hunted the same prey, and, in addition, as still happens today, the wolf also preyed on man's livestock, or even his children when they were lost and alone in the woods. No doubt these are some of the reasons behind man's aversion to the animal. Over time, terrifying fables told to keep children quiet developed into the most fantastic legends about "the big bad wolf" handed down from generation to generation.

It is astonishing to note the contradictions in the accounts of those who live in regions inhabited by this mythical predator. Strangely, it seems that women who encountered wolves reacted less fancifully than men and gave a more accurate account of wolves' behavior towards humans.

Wolves killed by hunters, professional or otherwise, were a coveted trophy, carried through the village and displayed in the main square. On show like this, everyone – women, old people and above all children – could come to see, touch or taunt them.

A woman from the Tuscan–Emilian Apennines in Italy, who boasted of two encounters with a wolf, would say, in a low voice, that she felt no fear and that the wolf looked at her for several seconds before making off. On the other hand, her husband would have nothing to do with these animals; to him they were harmful and dangerous, and all he wanted was to exterminate them.

Inevitably frictions occur where wolves live close to humans, whether on the mountains or in tiny villages. Yet some people manage to appreciate the importance of this wild species and to co-exist with it, or even benefit from it. They pursue their usual activities, such as pasturing their livestock, with the help of guard dogs that are sometimes protected with an anti-wolf collar. Nowadays, in France and Italy, the ravages of a predatory wolf are compensated by law.

In fact, there are two wolves: one is the real animal, the predator; the other – the better-known image – is a mythical wolf, subject of cruel and bloody legends. This fantastical image was forged during the Middle Ages and the animal gradually came to be associated with the very essence of the devil.

This traditional concept has forced the wolf to lead a very difficult life, hounded by persecutions, tracking and killings. There are men still living who used to be professional wolf-killers. Who were they? Cunning killers armed with guns who chased the animals systematically and pitilessly, sometimes totally eradicating them from their country. Tales of wolf-hunters and their exploits used to be a staple of evening gatherings, before they became stories for children. In many countries, when a wolf-hunter returned to the village with his trophy he would be loaded with gifts from the population, in addition to his official payment from the State. Some hunters became famous through the region, gaining wealth and social respectability. Given the period in question – the fairly recent past, when people had a different view of the wolf – their behavior is not reprehensible; no doubt these hunters were great wolf-connoisseurs. However, it is surprising to learn that until the early 1970s most countries still considered the wolf a dangerous

This photograph of the last wolf killed in Piedmont (Italy) dates from 1921. The hunters received a handsome reward for the animal, whose head was highly valued. The beast's body was paraded through the streets of Mondovì on a wagon, to the sound of a trumpet calling the alarm to attract the curious.

Whenever a wolf was killed a festival was organized. In those days, children felt a mixture of fear and curiosity about the animal, as well as a touch of contempt. Those feelings came to the fore when the beast was vanquished

animal that should be exterminated. For instance, in Italy wolves have been strictly protected since 1976, yet as late as 1971 forest rangers were still culling them by poison and hunters could slaughter them without restrictions.

This attitude can probably be explained by the difficulty of life in mountain villages, where the very harsh existence was imbued with a Manichean religious culture, in which Good was absolutely opposed to Evil.

As a result, stories of wolves are rich in symbolism. One of the most baneful, especially in Europe, was where the devil was personified in the form of a werewolf or lycanthrope, half-man, half-wolf. These terrifying creatures were supposed to live in the forests at night and to feast on human flesh. You could defend yourself from them if you knew their weaknesses: they could not climb more than three steps and were transfixed by the sign of the Cross. While lycanthropy is largely a myth, scientists now think that it may have originated in a genuine psychiatric illness, a sort of zooanthropic (man as animal) paranoia. However, beliefs are enduring and humans have always needed scapegoats.

Nevertheless there is a dual aspect to the symbolic value of the wolf: on the one hand dark and terrifying, the animal can also be benevolent and life-saving. In some cultures it accompanies

Guard dogs – like this Maremma sheepdog from Italy's Abruzzi region, or a Pyrenean mountain dog – are one of the most effective ways of protecting sheep from wolf attacks. These dogs are sometimes equipped with anti-wolf collars in iron or iron and leather, with enormous spikes to protect their necks in close fighting with a wolf.

souls to the hereafter. Hades, the Greek god of the Underworld, wore a wolf skin and the Etruscan god of death had the ears of a wolf.

This positive aspect of the wolf is stressed in the luminous character attributed to it by the fact that it can see in the dark, and its celestial aspect (for the Chinese, the star Sirius is a "wolf"). To the Mongols, the wolf represents the Sky and is the companion of the white deer, symbolizing the Earth: from their sacred union heroes such as Genghis Khan were born.

In Celtic culture, the wolf stands for kindness and loyalty since it loves and protects its kin. It guides those who venture into the world of the spirits, and comes to the aid of those in need. The wolf is the messenger of the goddess of "death in life". It serves as a companion to the land of the dead, guiding souls through the forests of the otherworld. In Native American cultures, such as that of the Blackfoot tribe, scouts were often called "wolves," referring to the animals' great skill in tracking their prey, and their fidelity, at the price of their life, to the complex society to which they belong. It was also thought that they could not be poisoned because their digestive system automatically expels all harmful substances (a self-defense system defeated by the powerful poisons created by modern chemistry). So the wolf symbolized the capacity to discover danger and to work for the good of the community, as well as the ability to find the right path through life.

Sometimes a wolf can only feed itself by attacking domestic animals, but the risks it runs during these encounters are very high. Only a well-publicized policy of paying compensation for damage done by wolves can smooth the cohabitation between shepherds and wolves, although it is very rare to find a shepherd who won't kill a wolf, if he gets the chance.

In Native American mythology, the gray wolf represents the figure of the master and the sage; its teeth are a talisman, ensuring courage and liberty.

Such beliefs also linger in Europe. For instance, in Italy it is thought that placing a little sachet filled with powdered wolf liver inside the cradle can protect and strengthen a newborn baby, or that wolf-skin puttees strengthen the legs of those who wear them. Likewise, throughout the world, man has always appropriated the appearance of his country's fiercest or rarest predator: there are tiger-men in India, jaguar-men in Latin America, lion-men in Africa, etc. This metamorphosis sometimes has shamanistic aims of vision and exploration, contact with the spirit and communication with the hereafter, but in most cases man takes the animal's skin to commit with impunity grave crimes in its name ... while the poor beast is, to say the least, probably less violent than man and certainly less cruel.

These are vestiges of an ancient mentality, but films, fables, and legends still feed the collective imagination with these fantastic and terrifying stories. In our time, however, we can contribute to re-establishing the truth, albeit with difficulty. It is true that fear of wolves seems to be ingrained in humans – like the fear of reptiles, hairy insects or rats. But nowadays people seem

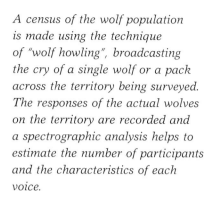

A census of the wolf population is made using the technique of "wolf howling", broadcasting the cry of a single wolf or a pack across the territory being surveyed. The responses of the actual wolves on the territory are recorded and a spectrographic analysis helps to estimate the number of participants and the characteristics of each voice.

to want to understand and question the received ideas of the past. It is time to speak of the wolf as it really is.

This does not mean that we should abandon the story of Little Red Riding Hood. It will retain its pleasingly mysterious and slightly scary charm and its happy ending – even for the wolf. In any case, it cannot harm the wolf. On the contrary, it is a chance to introduce the animal to children, who are inclined to dream and to let their imaginations roam, provided, of course, that they will understand the truth when the right moment arrives.

In any case, well before so much twaddle about the wolf was invented, man chose it as a life companion, selecting and educating it over thousands of years, transforming it into a dog. Today there are countless canine types throughout the world; from this point of view, it can be said that the wolf's true evolutionary success is this transformation, even if this is not strictly correct from a biological or scientific viewpoint.

Proud and loyal to its kin, the wolf is an important link in the world's ecosystems. Its presence in a territory, the result of a great capacity for adaptation even under difficult conditions where prey is scarce, indicates the quality of the habitat.

Nowadays dogs defend livestock against the attacks of their cousin the wolf, but they also help the survival of that species in difficult times. Wolves in populations reduced to tiny numbers have cross-mated with wild dogs, having no other means of reproducing themselves.

In recent times, wolf populations have increased globally and mating with dogs no longer takes place. When it lives outside human circles, the dog reverts to being the wolf's competitor for food and becomes fully integrated into the wild.

But who can foretell the future?

One thing is certain: the internal balance of the "man/dog/wolf" triangle will continue to be modified, in favor of one or other of the parties. But we now know that the wild cousin will always be with us and that its right to live free is indisputable. The triangle cannot be broken and each of us can contribute to the wolf's security.

Let us speak of it with respect and honesty and admire its qualities and its achievements.

Getting to know the wolf

A predator's life

What do we know about the wolf, except that we fear it and it looks like a large dog?

Naturally, everyone has heard of wolves but who has actually seen one?

The wolf is certainly familiar to us, and has been for hundreds of thousands of years. But what is it, really? How does it live? In the first place, it is a carnivorous "placental" mammal (not an omnivore, like man). Placenta nourishes the pups and helps them to grow during the first phase of their lives when they are protected in the belly of their mother. Not all mammals are placental: marsupials like the kangaroo or the Tasmanian devil, and *Monotremata* (egg-laying mammals) such as the *Ornithorhynchidae* (duck-billed platypus) are "aplacental" mammals.

The first mammals appeared on Earth around 195 million years ago in the Jurassic period; they were insectivores and were the

forerunners, after many evolutions and differentiations over millions of years, of all the mammalian orders that we know: primates, carnivores, cetaceans, etc.

In fact, from earliest times right down to our own day, many varied species of animals have struggled to survive on the resources and territories available to them. The necessity of survival leads to selection, of individuals as well as species. Together with the huge capacity for change inherent in life itself, this selection entails, century after century, significant modifications. So, within a species only the strongest individuals and – let us say– the most "cunning" survive. It is these and only these that unite to form a

From the tip of the nose to the end of the tail, a wolf measures between 40–50 inches (100–150 cm), and from the ground to the shoulder, when standing on all fours, its height ranges from 20–32 inches (50–80 cm). The heaviest specimens live in the colder regions of the northern hemisphere, where they can weigh up to 176 lbs (80 kg), the equivalent of an adult man.

The wolf as we know it today appeared on earth around 2 million years ago. Its first true ancestor belonged to the genus Cynodictis. It was more like a large weasel than a true wolf.

Wolves are digitigrade: they walk on their toes. The front paws have five digits (the dewclaw is higher than the others), the rear paws have four.

Uniquely, wolves regulate their temperature through the mucus membranes of the mouth and the surface of their lungs.

Wolves are at their most aggressive when feeding.

line of descent. Over time, this process may lead to the creation of a new species. From generation to generation, the shape and appearance of individual animals is transformed, the vital cycles evolve and are redefined. In this way, the species adapts to the evolutions of the surrounding environment, to climate modifications, available diet, coexisting or "enemy" species. This evolutionary capacity enables the species to last for centuries or millennia; without this ability, it would succumb and disappear. Extinction is not unusual in nature: 90 percent of

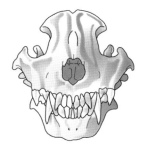

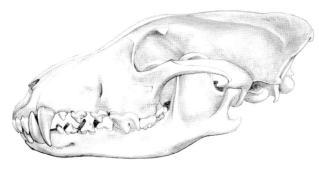

A sophisticated hunting machine

Whether the jaw is open or closed, the canine teeth, seen frontally, give an idea of the strength of the wolf's grasp on its prey. The orbital angle is an excellent way to distinguish the skull of a wolf from that of a dog. In dogs the angle is smaller (53°–60°). Powerful chewing muscles (masseter, pterygoid and temporal), attached to the bony structure of the skull, govern the wolf's complex chewing apparatus.

The canine teeth can grow to 1 1/2 inches (3.5 cm) in length and the extremely powerful jaws exert a pressure that has been estimated at 1500 lbs per square inch (100 g per square centimeter). While the canine teeth are used to seize prey, the molars, especially the carnassial teeth (upper fourth premolar and lower first molar), serve to shear the meat and gnaw the bones.

the species that once existed on earth have disappeared. Thanks to this slow, progressive evolutionary phenomenon, the first mammals living on insects 130 million years ago gave way around sixty-five million years ago to the first carnivorous fossils, the Creodonts. However, it took nearly another twenty million years before the ancestors of today's terrestrial carnivores appeared, notably those of the *Canidae* or canids, the wolf family and also that of jackals, coyotes and dingoes (the wild dogs of Australia).

In its present-day form, the wolf appeared on earth around two million years ago. Despite the fears and persecutions previously mentioned, its grace, strength, and beauty have always fascinated humans. It seems that from its first appearance *Homo sapiens* felt a special admiration for the wolf and its extraordinary abilities: a partially evolved wolf bone was discovered in a 14,000-year-old Paleolithic cave. From that time at least generations of humans devoted themselves to molding the wolf, its body, and its psychology until it evolved into a dog.

Wolves have a significant ability to cover long distances: they can travel 30 miles (50 km) a day.

The wolf's appearance and its social organization vary depending on the different geographical zones of their habitat. For example, weight and size differ considerably according to climate and territory. Wolves assemble in large packs where they have more space and, importantly, more resources.

The wolf may also seem larger and more impressive depending on whether it is in its winter or summer pelage (or coat); it molts twice a year. A wolf in its summer coat, seen in central European latitudes where wolves exist in greater density than their counterparts in southern regions, has a streamlined, supple body, with feet that appear large in relation to its overall size. Its external appearance is adapted to the habitat in which it lives, but its frame remains that of a tireless trotter.

Whether stepping about, trotting or running, the wolf does it "on tip-toes." Wolves are actually digitigrades, they stand or walk on their toes; when they are tracked for days on end, these are often the only sign of their presence in the territory. The color of the pelage is very variable and it is difficult for non-specialists to

In very hot weather wolves tend to rest in the shade of the forest. During winter, on the other hand, they protect themselves from the cold by hollowing out holes in the snow.

A wolf is covered and protected by two types of pelage: a thick, insulating undercoat called "ground fur," and a longer deeper-colored outer coat, typical of winter periods, the "guard hair." The wolf molts twice a year, in spring and fall.

To survive, the wolf needs to eat between 2–6 lbs (1–3 kg) of meat per day. But meals are not regular and, in case of scarcity or real famine, the largest wolves, those living in the far north, can eat up to 33–44 lbs (15–20 kg) at a time.

appreciate the subtle variations. Shades and tones differ greatly and are generally not uniform, although totally black or basically white specimens exist. The appearance of the pelage changes from summer to winter, when the coat is thicker and the colors deeper.

Wolves have another characteristic: they do not sweat and they regulate their temperature uniquely through breathing, so when it is very hot they tend to rest, protected in the shade of the forest. Their only true sweat glands are located on the foot pads and serve to inform other wolves of their presence by scent-marking.

The wolf's muzzle is elongated, its ears small and rounded. The jaw, with its forty-two powerful teeth and vigorous chewing muscles, is the wolf's principal attack mechanism. When you look at a wolf, just the sight of its canine teeth – jaw closed – is enough to give you an idea of the strength of its grip.

When wolves' dead and partly-devoured prey is found in a forest, it is possible to reconstitute the dynamics of the attack by analyzing all the indications left in the surrounding area. Take, for example, the case of an adult male deer weighing 462 lbs (214 kg) that researchers tracked wherever it went by a small radio-transmitter on its collar, like a cowbell. In the last months of its life, this old stag fell ill and was attacked and killed by three wolves that literally tore it to pieces over several meals, even gnawing the bones, while protected by a large hawthorn bush. The remains of their meal, which each wolf ate separately, were found hidden in the brambles. But what do wolves prey on? What do they eat? By nature the wolf is an opportunist. In ecological terms it can be defined as a super-predator. That means that it feeds on everything it can find on its territory: wild or domestic herbivores, rabbits, rodents, birds, reptiles,

The wolf's diet varies according to available prey. If it lives in a pack, it may attack an adult elk, but if it lives in a small group or alone, it confines itself to smaller prey, sometimes even amphibians or insects.

amphibians, even insects, but also (and this is the definition of a super-predator) other predators, such as foxes, badgers or even stray dogs. When it can find nothing better, it may even scavenge garbage and eat leftovers. Nor does it turn up its nose at small quantities of fruit, berries, and grasses.

The wolf's history is one of evolutionary success precisely because of its non-specialized diet, even though it is a predator. This success enables it to live practically throughout the northern hemisphere.

To survive in such different environments, spread over such a large territory, an animal needs to be gifted with remarkable intelligence and refined sensory equipment. The wolf's sense of smell and its hearing are highly developed, enabling it to gather a wealth of information such as we cannot imagine. One of the greatest experts in the species, David Mech, states that a wolf can scent the presence of a moose at 328 yards (300 meters) and that of a cow at almost a mile (1500 meters). Its ability to follow a scent while trotting along and to spot danger thanks to its sense of smell or its hearing make this animal master of a world that does not belong to us.

Within the territory there are special hunting zones. Wolves leave their resting place and set off in single file.

A wolf-hunt can be reconstructed by studying tracks in the snow, but only the discovery of the remains of prey can give an idea of the attack's true dynamic.

In the world's remaining wild places, the links between the wolf and its prey, and their confrontations, resemble those between lions and gazelles, with all the contacts and breaks that occur between the two parties in a typical day. Wolves often remain in visual contact with their prey, their mobile larder. When hunger begins to stimulate their hunting instinct, excitement mounts. Social orders ranging from submissive to dominant are confirmed: each wolf has a task, a role to play during the hunt. However, successes are few in comparison with the number of attempts; indeed, prey animals that live in close contact with a predator are familiar with their habits and are constantly on the alert since they "know" their lives are at risk. This is one of the reasons why wolves select their victims, attacking the most vulnerable: young animals or, in contrast, those that are old and ill, injured or isolated.

A wolf carefully evaluates its attack strategies and unless it is really hungry it will give up when the risk is greater than the chances of success. Take the case of the

wild boar, a favorite prey of the wolf in Italy and also in the south of France and Spain. Attacking an adult boar is dangerous, while the sow also becomes very aggressive when any of its young or other females are nearby. So the wolf prefers to tackle young males. At about one year old, young boars leave their mothers and the porcine matriarchal group; they have grown to a good size, they are relatively defenseless and inexperienced. This is when the wolf attacks them.

Apart from particular phases in its life (always less favorable) when an individual wolf finds itself alone, wolves live and hunt in packs. During hunting there may be competition between different packs, but never within individual packs. This is why social organization as well as the demarcation and defense of an "exclusive" hunting territory are so important for wolves' survival. In fact, where there is less human pressure and therefore more available prey, the wolf population stabilizes by subdivision of the space between neighboring packs. A pack will defend its territory against other packs, chasing them away if they do not respect the boundaries.

But how does a pack recognize another pack's territory? Wolves deliver a series of messages, written on the ground in visible and olfactory signs. In addition to "classic" marking techniques (urination and defecation,

also practiced by dogs and other animals) wolves use scent marking, through the glands between the toes and the contents of anal sacs: these little pouches secrete a substance produced by special glands, which may be deposited at the same time as feces. Nor should howling be forgotten; this signals the pack's presence to other packs that may be in the neighborhood or in transit. Having analyzed and begun to understand some aspects of the wolf's social structure in a territory that it knows to its paw-tips and is rich, as far as can be determined, in prey, let us now consider what goes on among wolves when they prepare for the hunt.

First we must dismiss the idea of bloodthirsty wolves or perfect hunting machines, capable of pursuing their prey for dozens of miles: not all attacks are successful, far from it.

Under ideal conditions, the wolf follows the logic of minimum effort for maximum gain. A wolf pack knows its territory from end to end and if it can, at least during part of the year, it will live in direct contact with prey animals. But it is not possible to define or to describe precisely or methodically the logic that makes different wolf packs throughout the world embark on the hunt. Observations of hunts in the wild are rare. Most have

When they scrape the ground with the scent glands between their toes (this is called "unearthing"), wolves signal their presence to other wolves visually and by smell. This is a way of marking the limits of their territory.

been carried out by aerial surveillance in North American territories; they have usually been partial observations and not all have been successful. Observers have generally encountered problems with the terrain: while much can be deduced from prints in the snow, it is rarely possible to grasp the strategy of the hunt. On the ground, it is difficult to establish whether wolf tracks were made minutes or an hour after those of the prey animal, whether they were made by wolves that were in full pursuit or simply prospecting for their quarry. Obviously, when an observer follows tracks that lead to the remains of the victim, with signs of struggle in the snow, an adequate reconstruction of events is possible.

The most likely theory is that wolves definitely follow strategies, but that their technique is essentially based on a chance encounter with a prey animal or with the scent it has left on the territory; if the traces are fresh, the wolves will go in search of their victim.

Wolves sometimes eat domestic livestock. They probably attack them by the neck, as they are easier prey than wild animals.

A pack of wolves wakes up. They are hungry and begin to show their appetite. There's a sense of tension in the air, it becomes sharper then grows into excitement, frenzy. The youngest wolves start to display active submission to their superiors. The wolves communicate with each other through different postures, indicating their hunger and their needs.

The inferior wolves in the pack's hierarchy start behaving like nursing pups to inform the dominant ones about their physical state, notably by muzzle-to-muzzle con-

tacts. At a certain moment, the wolves gather and begin to patrol their territory in search of prey. Within a territory there are special hunting grounds; to get to them, the wolves leave their resting place and travel in single file to save energy.

When their tracks in the snow are followed, places where individual wolves have fanned off can sometimes be spotted (this stage is often marked by sprays of urine). These are probably areas where logic and experience tell them there is a greater chance of encounter-ing prey and they disperse in order to comb a larger area simultaneously. By means of this exploration technique and their formidable olfactory capabilities, wolves scare out their prey, such as an elk or deer hidden in the vegetation, quietly chewing what little nourishment it has found in the woods during winter. The chase being launched, the wolves regroup and attack. In most cases, the prey animal reacts in one of three ways: it freezes, an attitude that seems to inhibit, at least temporarily, the aggression of the wolves, or it

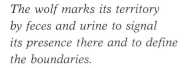

The wolf marks its territory by feces and urine to signal its presence there and to define the boundaries.

flees, and the wolves pursue. At this point, the prey's chances of survival are essentially down to its physical stamina and the determination of its predators. The pursuit may cover several hundred yards, sometimes several miles. The third possibility is that the prey will defend itself, and this is what the largest animals such as deer and elk will do, being big enough to take on a whole pack. Both in Europe and in North America, there are reports of deer defending themselves by using their hind hooves like a boxer uses his gloves.

When a wolf attacks, it tries to bite its prey from all angles, harrying it while trying to avoid kicks and jabs from horns. The myth of the wolf pursuing its victim and killing it instantly by seizing it by the neck is just more of the nonsense circulated about this animal. It is true that the prey is finished off like this, but only after fifteen minutes of struggle, many wounds, or because it is brought to its knees in the snow. In nature, a poor choice is paid for at the cost of life, and wolves live on the errors of their victims, their naiveté, their weaknesses, or their illnesses. They are these animals' natural selectors and, paradoxically, the species benefits from this.

Only the most wary animals, those with good sensory ability, good motor skills and an excellent knowledge of their territory, will succeed in escaping from wolves. The rest will succumb and their death prevents their "defects" being transmitted to their progeny.

Take, for instance, the case of a population of white-tailed deer that was subjected to the selective pressure of a predator such as a wolf: the result was that this species became better and better adapted to the conditions of a very harsh natural life.

Canis Lupus

The wolf and its territory

The wolf has adapted to the most extreme climates and the most difficult conditions. It has long learned how to co-exist with humans, and not as an enemy.

Wolf distribution throughout the world is "circumpolar Holarctic"; this means that wolves are – or were – to be found in all regions of the northern hemisphere, with the exception of tropical forests and desert regions, although there are smaller wolves in the Middle East that have adapted physically and physiologically to the harsh life of the desert.

On the North American continent, wolf populations are found between the 20th and the 80th northern parallel, extending to the limit of the land area. In Eurasia, habitat is limited only by the sea. Japan even had two wolf subspecies, *Canis lupus hattai*

Despite the persecutions it suffered in the past and to which it is still subject, the wolf is an example of biological success. Wolf populations exist in North America, Europe and Asia, in almost all types of environment.

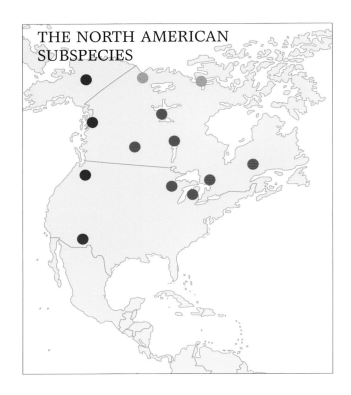

THE NORTH AMERICAN SUBSPECIES

- Canis lupus arctos (Arctic wolf or white wolf)
- Canis lupus baileyi (Mexican wolf)
- Canis lupus lycaon (Eastern timber wolf)
- Canis lupus nubilus (Great Plains wolf)
- Canis lupus occidentalis (Mackenzie Valley wolf)

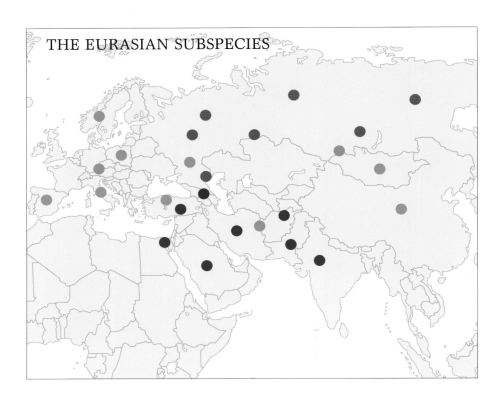

THE EURASIAN SUBSPECIES

- Canis lupus albus (Tundra wolf)
- Canis lupus arabs (Arabian wolf)
- Canis lupus lupus (Eurasian wolf)
- Canis lupus communis (Russian wolf)
- Canis lupus cubanensis (Caspian Sea wolf)

and *Canis lupus hodophilax*, on the islands of Hokkaido and Honshu, but they are now extinct.

Nowadays wolf population density is greatest in the most northerly zones, probably because relatively few humans live in these inhospitable regions. The further south you go in the more temperate zone, the more sporadic the wolf distribution; there are vast regions where no wolves are to be found, breaking the continuity of distribution areas and isolating different populations from each other. In Europe, until the nineteenth century, wolves lived wherever there were forests and food supplies, on the plains as well as in the mountains, except in Great Britain

and Denmark, where the species had already been extinct for one or two centuries at least. The wolf was relentlessly eliminated throughout Europe; special State bodies were dedicated to wiping it out, such as the French "Louveterie," a wolf-hunting corps. Thereafter the species disappeared from many Western European countries: it was extinct in Belgium and Western Germany from the end of the nineteenth century, in Luxemburg from 1903, and officially declared extinct in France in 1939. Today wolves survive in small isolated populations in Spain, Portugal and Italy, with a few specimens in Sweden and Norway. In Italy, wolves used to live everywhere, from Sicily to the Alps, except in Sardinia, but within several decades, due to the efforts of Sicilians and their *lupare* (sawn-off shotguns), of uncontrolled deforestation, of poisoned bait and the bloody work of professional wolf hunters, the species was almost completely eradicated. Today the bulk of the European wolf population is in Eastern Europe, probably thanks to the huge empty spaces of the former Soviet Union.

The beginning of the twentieth century marked a turning-point: man's attitude towards the wolf and the environment in general changed considerably, and over the past thirty years the situation has improved. Thanks to several international conventions – the Bern Convention, CITES (Convention on International Trade in Endangered Species of Wild Fauna and Flora) and community directives relating to critical environments – to which many countries subscribe, the wolf and its vital habitats are beginning to gain protection. Woods have been restocked with the wolf's natural prey, and in some countries the State has decided to pay compensation for damage caused by its incursions on livestock. In addition, awareness campaigns have moderated the image of the terrible predator in the collective imagination and highlighted its genuine ecological role.

Distribution of the Canis lupus *species*

Canis lupus lupus

Canis lupus lupus *is the wolf subspecies that lives in Europe and most of Asia, with several populations isolated from one another. Geographical isolation* *is one of the factors that influence variations in the wolf's appearance and genome, leading to the emergence of a subspecies.*

The wolves of the Italian Apennines have been much studied and analyzed. Some of their characteristics, such as black bands on the front paws, a reddish undercoat the color of beech leaves in the fall, and strongly developed hindquarters, have led researchers to define them as a subspecies.

When humans started to abandon mountainous areas, the wolf, a wily opportunist, immediately took advantage and began a timid re-colonization of central European territories; Germany has a few wolves that came from the Czech Republic or Poland to the east, and the Swedish population is beginning to grow, even though it remains isolated. In Western Europe, in more than a score of countries with wolf populations, and for which figures are available, it has been noted that numbers are increasing in eight countries and are stable in nine others; there are only three situations that show a slight decline, and three countries where evolution is unknown. The total number of wolves in Europe (excluding the former Soviet Union) may be estimated at more than 14,000 and there are in excess of 70,000 in North America. In Asia the situation is hard to establish: wolf populations are protected only in Israel, are fragmented and poorly known.

The specific name for the wolf, *Canis lupus*, covers all the subspecies of wolves throughout the world. Bypassing the simple classification, wolves can be considered as a "polytypic" species, made up of numerous populations that are more or less isolated from each other, and differentiated by appearance, weight, and dietary habits. They can be classified into several subspecies: *Canis lupus lupus, Canis lupus arctos, Canis lupus arabs, Canis lupus baileyi...* Each of these names embraces populations that share more or less consistent characteristics.

Canis lupus arctos

The Arctic wolf, canis lupus arctos, has a creamy white pelage and ears that are relatively small and rounded. It lives above the 80th northern parallel, showing the species' enormous capacity for adaptation.

Canis lupus albus

The Tundra or Siberian wolf, canis lupus albus, here photographed in summer, is another classic example of adaptation to cold climates. In winter, its coat turns a silvery light grey, and grows thicker as protection from the harsh temperatures of the Siberian tundra.

Nowadays, Canis lupus lupus *encompasses not only the European wolf (above) but also the Mongolian* wolf *(opposite), formerly considered to be a member of the chanco subspecies.*

There are various theories establishing the numbers of wolf subspecies worldwide: estimates range from 32–38, 15, or even 6–8. It may be simpler – perhaps over-simplification – to divide them into two groups: forest wolves and tundra wolves.

Without dwelling on the characteristics that distinguish one subspecies from another, it is useful to consider these subspecies from the standpoint of their biological value, their shape and their capacity to adapt to the diversity of the natural world.

The most obvious example is that of the Eurasian Tundra or Siberian wolf (*Canis lupus albus*) that lives in the arid permafrost of the Siberian tundra. Its coat is the color of the ground on which it lives, light gray with silvery reflections and a few touches of black and rust; the fur is very dense, as protection from the cold. Its ears are small and rounded, a clear sign of adaptation to the extreme climates in which it lives, following – as do other species – the rule defined by environmentalist Charles Bergman: among mammals living in different

Canidae (canids)

Canids have remarkable structural homogeneity, as seen among different subdivisions of the family; they are often sociable, efficient hunters; they are curious, exploratory, and culturally adaptable; they are digitigrade, with five toes on the front paws and four on the rear ones. Their claws do not retract, allowing them to dig but not to seize prey. They live in all latitudes and their dentition is characterized by long canines and well-defined carnassial teeth.

Canis aureus *(Golden jackal)*

The golden jackal is a slender, long-legged canid, measuring 26–40 inches (65–105 cm), and weighing 15–33 lbs (7–15 kg). This opportunistic omnivore feeds on carrion and on mammals, from small rodents to gazelles, but also on fruit, insects and invertebrates. Of the three known species of jackals, the golden jackal – although considered an endangered species – is the most widespread, its habitat extending from Africa to southern Asia.

Alopex lagopus *(Arctic fox)*

The arctic fox looks very like the common fox; however, it is smaller, with shorter ears and muzzle. There are two subspecies; one has a predominantly white pelage, the other may have tints of silvery grey, blue or chestnut brown. These foxes live exclusively in arctic regions and are active throughout the year. In summer, they feed off insects, rodents, fish, and seabirds; in winter, they eat arctic hares and scavenge the leftovers of polar bears. Lemmings are their most common prey, captured by whisking them out of the snow with an agile bound.

Vulpes vulpes *(Red fox)*

With more than sixty subspecies, this is the most widespread of the nine species of common fox. The red fox is another star of the canid family, although its way of life differs from that of the wolf: its survival strategies entail a solitary existence. It hunts in the evening and at night and prefers small and medium prey, since it does not have to feed a pack.
Foxes sometimes follow wolf tracks in the snow, taking identical routes as well as foraging for the wolves' leftovers.

Nyctereutes procyonoides
(Raccoon dog)

This canid, widespread in East Asia, is of medium to small size, with a large body and a small head. It measures 24–28 inches (60–70 cm), with an 8-inch (20-cm) tail. Black patches around the eyes give it the look of a raccoon; it has a short tail and legs and a bushy coat.
It is found in areas where there is plenty of water and is fond of fish, which it captures with quick flicks of the paw, a skill that has earned it the nickname 'fishing dog'.

Chrysocyon brachyurus
(Chrysocyon, Maned wolf, or lobo-guará (Portuguese: Guará Wolf)

The maned wolf has the muzzle and ears of a fox and the dimensions of a wolf. Its long legs help it to move with agility when hunting its prey in the long grass of the South American prairies of Argentina, Bolivia, Paraguay, Uruguay, and Brazil.

latitudes, the heaviest animals live in the north. In fact, a high body mass helps it to conserve heat. Its paws are smaller and rounded, in order to limit the extremities' exposure to cold, although – and this is the only exception to the rule – the legs of the Tundra wolf are rather long to help it follow constantly moving prey.

At the other extreme we have a very small wolf, weighing around 40 lbs (18 kg), living in an equally extreme environment, that of the Arabian peninsula in and around Egypt. This is the subspecies *Canis lupus arabs*, which, confirming Bergman's rule, has a heat-dispersing body surface, with larger ears and shorter fur. Clearly, its habits are adapted to the climate: in summer it is active at the beginning and end of the day; only in winter is it seen in the middle of the day.

Between these two extreme examples of wolves, there is a whole range of variants, sometimes called subspecies, which hybridize amongst each other on the edges of their territories and are differentiated by certain constant characteristics.

To add to the confusion surrounding species subdivision – still poorly understood and little clarified in scientific circles – it should be noted that the domestic dog and the red wolf, respectively *Canis familiaris* and *Canis rufus*, are not necessarily different species to *Canis lupus* since they retain the ability to interbreed and share their genetic heritage by giving birth to fertile offspring.

Although solitary predators do exist, wolves generally live in a pack, sharing a territory with several others. In America there may be up to thirty-five animals in a pack, but in Eurasia, the average ranges from five to ten wolves.

The wolf's build is that of a typical trotter; however it can cover up to 40 miles (64 km) per hour.

Following a line that characterizes the principal subspecies of the New World and the Old, the current classification scheme is largely based on the following subspecies.

Five subspecies exist on the American continent: *Canis lupus arctos*, commonly known as the arctic wolf, basically lives in the Arctic, from above the 70th parallel to above the 80th, on the limits of the landmass, where the land is covered with snow and ice for most of the year, except for a brief summer period. Arctic wolves are well adapted to this frozen habitat. They have a creamy white fur that camouflages them in the environment, and other adaptations like those of the Tundra wolf (*Canis lupus albus*). The scarcity of prey forces them to roam over immense territories to survive, hunting musk oxen, arctic hares, lemmings, caribou, and birds of passage. They make their dens in rock outcroppings, caves, or depressions in the ground; the mother gives birth to two or three pups, about a month later than southern wolves, the small litter being the most that can be reared in such extreme conditions.

Fur color is not always consistent, especially among the pups, where variations ranging from white to black are seen. Left, a specimen of the most common color, also seen in adults, of the Mackenzie Valley wolf, the American wolf belonging to the occidentalis *subspecies.*

Canis lupus baileyi, also known as the Mexican wolf, is the smallest North American gray wolf, weighing 50–88 lbs (23–40 kg). It was close to extinction until protective measures were taken during the 1970s. Thanks to a preservation program, the species has been reintroduced in Arizona and New Mexico. Typically, the Mexican wolf preys on white or crossbred deer, elks, rabbits and small mammals.

Canis lupus lycaon, the Eastern timber wolf, was the first gray wolf species to be recognized in the United States where it lives in the eastern regions and in the

Canadian south-west. Like all wolves, it is a social animal that communicates through body language, scent marking and voice. Despite availability of habitat and prey, natural re-colonization is unlikely due to extensive human infrastructure and large urbanized areas. Naturalists have tried to reintroduce a small population in the Adirondacks, in Oregon, but in early 2000 a survey of the resident population showed that the inhabitants of the region were deeply divided about this project. Before the classification scheme was modified, it was estimated that timber wolf distribution extended to

The wolf's sense of hearing and smell are highly developed, making it a formidable hunter. In reality wolves are not bloodthirsty predators and spend much of their time resting quietly in the security of the pack.

Minnesota, Michigan and Wisconsin, but this is now thought to be another subspecies, *Canis lupus nubilus*.

Canis lupus nubilus or Great Plains wolf is the most common subspecies of the gray wolf in the Continental United States. The extent of its territory depends on the availability of its prey, basically Virginia (white-tailed) deer, moose, beaver, hares, small birds and mammals. Nowadays it is found in the eastern region of the Great Lakes, with the following populations: 216 in Michigan, 29 in Isle Royale (Lake Superior), 266 in Wisconsin, and 2450 in Minnesota (data from 1997–8). During the 1920s, the Great Plains wolf was thought to be extinct, but a small nucleus not recognized as Plains wolves survived in north-eastern Minnesota, near Ontario. Since the end of the 1970s, the population has increased regularly and the Great Plains wolf is no longer considered critically endangered, at least not in that region.

The last of the American subspecies, scientific name *Canis lupus occidentalis*, generally known as the Mackenzie Valley wolf, is a large wolf that lives in Alaska, in northern Canada and in the Rocky Mountains; this was the subspecies reintroduced into

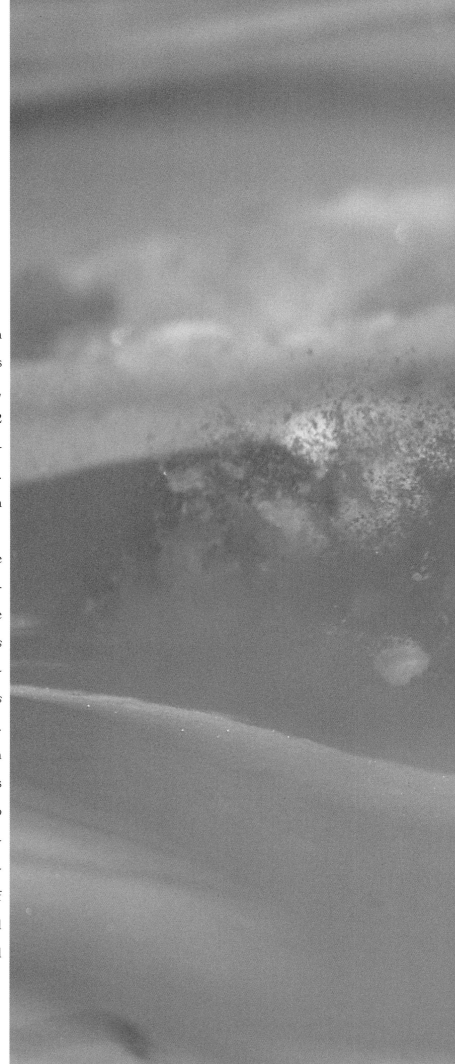

Yellowstone National Park (YNP) in Idaho. It can weigh up to 148 lbs (67 kg) and the color of its pelage ranges from white through gray to black, the most common colors. Packs average 6–12 wolves but can reach thirty. The largest population, some 7000–10,000 wolves, lives in Alaska. It prey includes moose, bison, caribou, mountain goats, salmon, and rodents of all kinds.

There are also five wolf subspecies on the Eurasian Continent – or six if *Canis lupus pallipes*, the Indian wolf, is considered a separate subspecies and not merged with *Canis lupus arabs*; we follow the second option. The characteristics of *Canis lupus albus* and *Canis lupus arabs* have been described earlier (p. 48 and p. 57). *Canis lupus lupus* is the typical Eurasian wolf found in France, Italy and Spain; nowadays the subspecies *Canis lupus desertorum*, *chanco* and *campestris* have been merged into this classification, extending the Eurasian wolf's territorial distribution (that already included parts of Asiatic Russia) east as far as Mongolia, Nepal and China, and south to Pakistan, Iran and Afghanistan.

A family group

These photographs show moments in the life of a typical family group of Italian wolves. The sequence was taken several years ago, in the Foreste Casentinesi National Park,

Monte Falterona, Campigna, during a scientific research project.
As well as determining the number of individuals in the zone and their use of the territory, the project

studied the wolf's dietary preferences. It seems that, given the choice, wolves prefer to feed off wild animals rather than domestic livestock.

Opposite: *two young brother wolves, one white and one black, make a good demonstration of the way in which the color of the pelage can vary, especially among Mackenzie Valley wolves, going from one extreme to the other and including all shades in between.*

The assurance and inner tranquility of the wolf's gaze are fascinating.

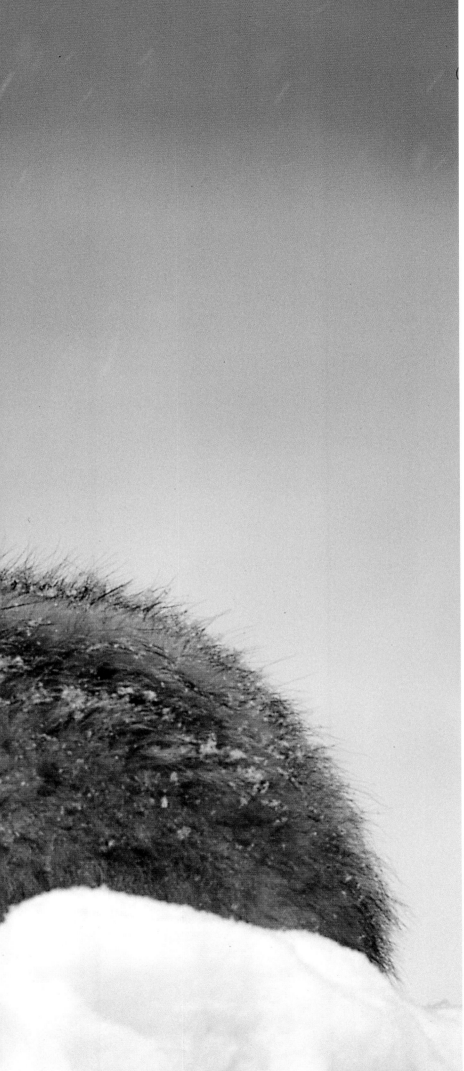

Two images of wolves in repose. Among wolves, periods of rest alternate frequently with periods of activity. When it is cold, they dig holes in the snow where they can shelter, reducing the bodily surface exposed to the elements.

Canis lupus communis is the Russian wolf, and, together with the American *occidentalis* sub-species, is one of the largest gray wolves.

The last of the Eurasian subspecies is *Canis lupus cubanensis*, the Caspian Sea wolf that appears to live in the territories between the Caspian and the Black Sea; until recently its existence was unknown.

No doubt the general picture will remain some-what confused, but essentially the one thing that interests us and that never ceases to aston-ish us is the immense capacity for adaptation of this persecuted species that finally, in a modi-fied and familiar form – the dog – entered many millions of our homes. Consequently, the wild wolf that our ancestors considered their equal should be respected and defended. First, it is important to get to know the wolf and to forget all the silly things that have been said about it.

This adolescent specimen of the Eurasian wolf is watching us. It still has all its life before it, and it is up to us whether it will live peacefully as a super-predator at the top of the food chain, or as a scavenger, forced to search for food in our piled-up garbage.

The pack
Wolves are social animals

For a long time, it was thought that the wolf was a solitary animal. The expression "lone wolf" means someone who works alone and shuns the company of others.

But wolves live in packs, and when a wolf is separated from the pack and lives alone, its existence becomes harsher, more difficult, and dangerous. In general, it is once-dominant old wolves that are chased from the pack after losing their supremacy, or they may decide to spend some time living alone. However, a young wolf may also experience a short or longer period of solitude. It lacks the experience an old wolf would have accumulated to enable it to cope, and this period is often fatal. If the wolf is healthy and manages to survive, it will find a companion; the couple will unite and found their own pack. They will find their own territory, marking it with visual and olfactory signs and defending it against other packs or solitary wolves, since this is where the pups will be brought up and where the pack will develop its organization and its hierarchy.

In environments with sufficient resources to feed them all, wolves live in large packs. Life within a pack improves survival chances for each individual and enables them to hunt large prey. Wolves get very excited when they embark on the chase, pursuing the prey together and attacking it from all angles.

Establishing hierarchies

Depending on its social rank, each wolf in the pack asserts itself by communicating through body language and its muzzle. The muzzle is not only a weapon but also a specialized instrument exchanging through scenting chemical information with other wolves. Inspection of the anogenital region leaves the animal stretched on the ground naked.

In Western Europe, where territories are fragmented and urbanized, wolf packs are smaller and are typically the size of a human family. Father and mother – the alpha or dominant couple – are usually the only pack members allowed to breed. All the rest are brothers and sisters who play together but who also tussle with each other, sometimes roughly, to gain a superior position in the hierarchy. A "pack of wolves" is an expression used to describe a fiercely aggressive group of humans but it has little to do with a real pack of wolves (at least in European countries). It is true that when wild prey is scarce, the pack may become more enterprising and aggressive and may attack flocks of sheep or other livestock, but, normally, wolves keep to themselves, avoiding contact with humans, and are no danger to them. In other regions, such as Alaska or the vast steppes of Eastern Europe, packs are much larger, because of the wider territories that they dominate. Several couples may have pups, social organization of the packs is much more complex, and wolves may sometimes be dangerous to humans.

The wolf is a social animal, and this sociability governs everything it does while it lives within the pack. Being together, sharing smells, a territory, prey, cohabiting

For fun or for real

Play, especially among the young, but also between couples, is an important part of the interaction between wolves. Adults may display tenderness with gentle nips, but when necessary they will assert their position in the hierarchy with great determination.

within a hierarchy imposed by experience and strength: such is life in the pack. The bond is strong and each animal has its own social position; this marks it out and may evolve over time. Living in a pack gives security and allows the animal to develop and to identify itself as an individual within the group. Pack life increases the chances of survival. A solitary wolf is forced to venture beyond the territorial boundaries set

Sometimes lower-ranking wolves in the hierarchy will submit to the dominant ones by licking their muzzles. This behavior is typical during a gathering or in the moments before the pack embarks on a hunt. Through this oral contact the dominant animals can assess how hungry the pack is.

by well-defined packs. A young wolf takes great risks in entering unknown territory, as it is obliged to hunt alone to feed itself. Such a wolf, intruding on occupied territories, may be treated with considerable violence by pack members. Outside the hunt, wolves can be extremely aggressive to intruders, those banished from the pack, and to other canids.

Within the pack, relations between wolves are very correct, and quarrels or frictions are generally resolved in a ritual fashion, rarely going as far as physical con-

frontation. However, territorial violation, even by a small dog trespassing in a "reserved" zone, may provoke a brutal response. The wolf will defend its zone, fiercely attacking the stranger that fails to recognize warning signals. It will savage it, seizing it by the neck between its jaws. The neck region is particularly significant for all canids. When pups are young, the mother or father lifts and carries them by the neck. This behavior is replicated in the hierarchic rituals of the pack: a dominant wolf will assert itself by seizing the offender by the

In communication between individual wolves, submissive signals may be voluntarily displayed by the inferior animal (this is called active submission) or they may be enforced by the dominant or alpha wolf (passive submission). In the photograph to the right, the dominant wolf rather aggressively asserts its superiority over the submissive one that lies on its back, legs in the air, utterly at the mercy of the alpha animal.

neck, raising it off its front legs and holding it with no support for its rear quarters. An adult wolf that has been treated like this is marked for life and often loses its place in the hierarchy.

The wolf's daily life is punctuated by action, by alternating periods of rest and forays, as well as by constant communication between pack members. The pack can be considered as a unit, a single body where the head is represented by the dominant individuals. All the others are submissive and inferior within the hierarchy.

This type of social organization may seem rigid but it ensures cohesion and coordination of behavior, which in turn enables the pack to exist and to prosper. Amongst canids, social communication is mainly by olfactory canals and very sophisticated behavioral patterns. The life of the pack is regulated by dominations and submissions, by looks and the language of body, ears, shoulders and tail, and by facial expressions. A wolf cannot dissemble: it is either dominant or submissive.

Aggression

Aggression is a basic element in wolves' lives. It is not always shown explicitly, but when feeding, ranking order is imposed by all possible means of expression.

Cooperation between wolves is essential when in pursuit of large prey. Each moment of their life within the pack is lived as a team. Sometimes several wolves will dominate another wolf at the same time, or they will take advantage of the submissiveness exacted by the alpha wolf by taking its place when it moves away from the lower-ranking animal.

Howling

Howling is one of the chief social activities within the pack. With wolves, howling signifies different things: defending their territory, communicating with other packs, or calling the wolves of the pack together. After an encounter, along with submissions and lickings, the pack sometimes howls to calm their frenzy and release tensions. When they howl, wolves place themselves in different positions so that their voices ring out over all the surrounding territory.

The wolf's vocal repertoire includes growling, barking, yapping and yelping. Each sound has its own meaning and is used to reinforce behavior. An alpha wolf asserts active domination over an inferior by growling, which reinforces its significance and explains that it has had enough. On the other hand, when a pack communicates with another pack they howl, and this is one of the most eerie and mythical sounds in animal life.

The structure of the pack runs in hierarchical lines between males, females, and yearling pups. The dynamism and complexity of communication within this ranking order are due to a system of complementary behavior made up of body-language, sounds, and scent signals, although not all of these signals are displayed by all wolves.

It is sometimes sufficient for an alpha wolf to assert its will or impose a choice by a look or a simple gesture. The idea that the dominant animals listen to their subordinates is an attractive but typically human interpretation. Each contributes to the wellbeing of the pack, during the hunt as well as in looking after the pups. The basic structure of the pack is the family unit, but the number of individuals within it varies, essentially depending on available food and the type of prey on which the wolves feed. The wolf's reproductive strategy has the advantages of stability within the environment: it watches over its pups, which are never too numerous – between two and five per year – and spreads

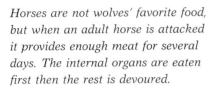

Horses are not wolves' favorite food, but when an adult horse is attacked it provides enough meat for several days. The internal organs are eaten first then the rest is devoured.

over the territory like an oil-slick. Where space and resources permit, several territories may run alongside each other. This is why the number of wolves in a pack can vary over time.

There are small packs, consisting of three to five wolves, parents and pups, such as in Italy or France. In these, first the male then the female yearlings disperse from the group and set out in search of new territories. Or there are enormous packs of thirty-five wolves, typically in North American forests, which include several generations of descendants plus uncles and aunts, just like a large family.

Packs communicate between themselves by means of scent markings and vocalizations. The wolf's vocal repertoire includes growling, barking, yapping and yelping, and when one pack communicates with another pack, they howl. Howling is one of the most disturbing and evocative sounds in wildlife: it has curdled the blood of generations of humans!

Howling is a great moment of collective expression, the culminating point of wolves expressing their sociability. The pack leader or its mate leads the song, and then the other members of the clan join in with an exultant chorus that gradually dies down until only the voice of the pack leader and its mate are heard. This community singing is an important social occasion within the pack; it reinforces its coherence and cohesion. Seeing four or five wolves howling their presence to the world is an extraordinary spectacle. Wolves in a group do not howl without reason, but as a result of certain events.

Wolves consume most of their kill and when the flesh has been eaten the remains are torn apart and the bones contested by several members of the pack. Each wolf makes off with the piece it has snatched and gnaws it undisturbed.

Young Wolves

Within the pack, behavioral dynamics follow hierarchical lines between males, females, or pups. Among the young the boundary between play and reality is often slight.

Following double-page spread: *Periods of activity frequently alternate with periods of rest. Wolves are basically carnivorous predators and* *their digestion lasts 6–8 hours. When their stomachs are full, they can allow themselves to rest, tranquilly stretched out to digest: unlike their* *prey, wolves need not fear being attacked by other animals and they probably live a quieter life, protected by the group to which they belong.*

Howling is used, for example, to signal the transition from inaction to action, but it is also employed on many other occasions. In every case, it is preceded by a joyful "group ceremony" during which the wolves assemble frantically with a growing excitement that culminates in choral howling. Howling is liberating; it energizes each individual and releases tensions. Howling can also be sadder and weaker, but if there are neighboring packs of wolves, it is always undertaken with some vigor.

At mating time, two- or three-month-old pups can sometimes be heard trying out their howling, skillfully guided by their father, who then ends it with a simple, circular "voice movement", like the leader of an orchestra. And – amazingly – the pups fall silent.

The "territorial-defensive" meaning of this vocalization has been widely documented. But howling also serves to communicate a position and to reunite the group after a hunt or to orient and reassure the pups when the adults are far away. By contrast, solitary wolves tend not to reveal their presence and therefore rarely howl, only in exceptional cases or when they need to defend their prey.

Strict discipline

*Submissive wolves show their social
ranking during a confrontation
by keeping their ears low, the tail
between their legs and by lowering
their hind quarters to shield their
anogenital region from being sniffed
by the dominant wolf.*

To experience stimulated wolf howling close up is always very fascinating and impressive. On starry and silent nights, in virgin territories with no light or acoustic pollution, it is possible to stimulate wolves into howling. You depart in two groups; the first gives the signal and the other records the eventual responses. It is always moving to hear in return the chorus of howls from a pack of wolves; the spectacle – perhaps it should be called the concert – becomes almost unbelievable if another pack joins in, and then a third! However, while howling is the supreme moment of dialogue between wolves (within the pack and to the outside world), communication within the pack is extremely important and ongoing.

Observing two wolves, it is not difficult to see and understand the communication between them, which is made up of visible attitudes conveyed by body-language, the muzzle and the tail. On the other hand, it is not possible to explore the scent signals, although it is known that certain regions – such as the anogenital region – are important transmitters of information.

In one-to-one relations, wolves react differently depending on their social position. Dominant wolves and the lowest-ranking ones apart, the behavior of other wolves in the pack is more submissive than dominant. The position of the ears, the position and size of the tail, depending on the bristle, the expression of the muzzle

Domination is sometimes exerted in the presence of other wolves, and with their participation.

The submissive animal crouches on the ground in a clearly inferior position.

and the display of teeth and tongue combine
with general body-posture, expression, and the
raising of the hairs from the back of the neck
down to the upper end of the tail. Taken
together, it is a complex group of elements con-
veying a state of being, a social position.
Dominant wolves carry themselves proudly,
with a firm step and steady gaze; the tail is held
high, lightly curved at the tip, and inflated; the
ears are erect and forward, breathing is easy,
controlled, and confident.

The behavior of submissive wolves is much less
confident; the tail – held low to the side or
between the legs to protect the anogenital
region – twitches nervously and brushes the
ground. The hindquarters are unsteady on the
legs and emphasize the low position of the tail
in the most difficult moments of confrontation,
during which even the knees bend. Submissive
animals will leap, lowering the ears and twisting
the body in a backwards rotation, as if impelled
by a superior force, to roll over, legs in the air.
Lying on the back is a recognizable attitude of
total submission, one that imitates the pup's
first stages of life when its mother would lick
and nibble its abdomen to stimulate defecation.

Riding-up

Riding-up is not genuinely submissive behavior since the wolf being ridden rarely displays a subordinate attitude. This position, where one wolf leans with its front paws on the other's back, is very common among pups; among adults it is probably a way of demonstrating social privilege to the rest of the pack. Active domination (right), on the other hand, clearly represents a relationship problem between two wolves.

There are two kinds of submissive behavior: active submission and passive submission. The first comprises several behavioral scenarios, or rather a whole range of different nuances of the same scenario. It can be indicated by a simple sniffing of the dominant animal's muzzle, with tail-waving (as a peace signal), or by licking and nibbling, the body tucked – hindquarters lowered, tail between the legs – and leaning towards the mouth of the dominant animal like a lover. If the alpha wolf is well-disposed, it appears rather absent-minded; sometimes, when active submission is displayed before a gathering ceremony, it seems almost irritated and holds its muzzle high. Passive submission, on the other hand, is not sponta-

neously displayed behavior but results from an emergency situation or confrontation with an adversary. Here the wolf lays itself open, exposed, its anogenital region presented for olfactory inspection, its neck vulnerable. Sometimes several wolves will simultaneously exert domination over a weaker individual, or young wolves will do it in play. Other wolves may take advantage of the submission exacted by the dominant wolf, taking its place when it moves away from the submissive one. Wolves' complex society is regulated by simple, direct rules: the law of the strongest wins. But the strongest must also be a good leader, capable of making good choices, especially when food is scarce.

The pair and the pups

In training for the hunt

Two solitary individuals,

male and female,

meet and court.

If the courtship is successful,

the wolves will mate.

With the first litter,

the pair becomes a pack.

Every year the birth of new pups involves all members of the pack. Reproduction is a major event for wolves: for three months of the year the principal activities of the pack-family revolve around the protection, weaning, and education of the pups. Wolves' breeding period occurs at the end of winter, between the end of February and early March, but the reproductive cycle actually lasts through the year, the average time the parents devote to caring for their little ones.

Looking after their progeny involves enormous expenditure of energy on the part of the parents. The exact details of wolves' reproduction are still largely unknown, but knowledge in this area has progressed over the past few years. It has been estab-

Communication between male and female during the mating season precedes lengthy stages of courtship.

lished that their reproductive strategy encompasses four phases: courtship, the actual mating, birth and the raising of the litter.

It all begins with the courtship, which is a bit like a trial-run before mating. During this stage the wolves go through a whole series of highly ritualized behavior. This first stage, lasting about a month, is essential so that the participants recognize each other, both as members of the same species and as potential partners. Wolves, especially dominant ones, live in pairs and a well-matched couple may stay together for a long time, sometimes until death. Mating between two wolves that do not know each other is stimulated by hormones released by the female as pheromones when she is in estrus (heat) At this point she and her potential mate will spend some time together. They begin by scenting each other, then howling and playing together, trotting or walking along, depending on their state of excitement. Normally only the dominant pair in a pack will

Courtship

Courtship is essential preliminary behavior before breeding and it lasts around a month, generally between mid-February–March, or later among wolves living in northerly regions. During this time the two wolves are very active, displaying a range of very tender and playful behavior; the female often dances around the male, jumping up and displaying her genital area. The male will sniff and lick this part of her anatomy with increasing frequency until they mate. This courtship behavior may also occur among wolves of different social ranking, although in such cases it is rare for actual coupling to take place. Male and female finish their mating in an "end-to-end" posture, also seen in dogs.

winter pelage		summer pelage						winter pelage			
March	April	May	June	July	August	September	October	November	December	January	February
estrus	gestation	lactation		pup				young wolf			

The pups grow up

The table above illustrates the wolves' life cycle over the year. The females come into estrus once a year (from January to March depending on the latitude, that is from the end of winter in the northern hemisphere): birth and suckling therefore take place at the beginning of the warmer season, following a gestation period lasting around two months. Suckling may also last this long although weaning can start after three weeks. Growth is very rapid: two-month pups already have great muscular strength; at six months they will follow the pack out hunting.

breed, although in large packs other wolves may attempt to mate, sometimes successfully impregnating a female. In such cases, however, the pregnant alpha female may attack the other female, sometimes even killing her. The female comes into heat – more technically, into estrus – once a year, between January and March in the case of the wolves of the northern hemisphere of whatever subspecies.

However there is some evidence that climactic and environmental factors, as well as latitude, influence the date of estrus among North American wolves: wolves that live further north reproduce later than those living in southern regions. In Italy, wolves reproduce after mid-March and, despite a latitudinal distribution varying by around 6° (from 38°9' to 44°8'), this period remains much the same for the whole population of the peninsula.

Wolves belong to the order of carnivores and are placentary mammals. The placenta protects the embryo then the fetus throughout the gestation period, and it is crucial for the exchange of nutritive substances between the mother and the litter. In mammals, the fertilized egg lodges at varying depth in the uterus. In addi-

The litter

During their first two weeks of life, the pups are blind and helpless. They cannot regulate their body temperature precisely, so they stay inside the den, in direct contact with their mother.

Mother and pups

The bond that develops between the mother wolf and her pups is particularly intense, especially during the first months of life. The other pack-members also share in the rearing of the cubs. The males – especially the mate – will bring food to the female after birth, and the females will help to care for the little ones.

During their first few months, the wolf pups stay close to the den, with periods of activity alternating with rest periods, especially during the hottest time of day.

Mother Love

*The pups show a strong need
for affection even if their developing
character quickly leads them t
o manipulate their relationship
with their siblings. In this way they
become part of a separate hierarchy
from the rest of the pack.*

Female wolves have six nipples distributed along the milk-line typical of mammals. Their milk is very nourishing and helps the cubs to grow rapidly; they can gain up to 3 1/2 lbs (1.5 kg) a week.

tion, depending on the orders of placentary mammals in question, the placenta, which starts out as chorionic villi, diversifies in various ways during the successive phases of development.

The gestation period lasts around two months. The female wolf's uterus is bipartite (it is divided into two parts) and on average contains three to six fetuses that are born blind and helpless in the darkness of the den. Fifteen to twenty-five days before giving birth, the female digs a den or arranges one in a rocky outcrop or in a cavity beneath a tree, anywhere within reach of water. When the pups are born, she cleans them with her tongue and pushes them towards her nipples. Like many mammals, the mother eats the placenta and cuts the umbilical cord with her teeth.

The cubs are covered with a thick, almost black, down but their ability to regulate their body temperature is very feeble. It seems that they are also deaf and have almost no sense of smell. They are cared for by their mother, who warms them and feeds them, while their

The young wolves start to eat meat quite early on, initially pre-chewed and pre-digested. When their milk teeth have strengthened they will tear the meat off prey provided by their parents.

Right and following double-page spread: *Young wolves' first months of life are characterized by play and curiosity about everything around them. During this phase – even if they are rarely left alone – the pups may, in their turn, become the prey of other animals.*

father or other members of the pack, in their turn, look after the mother. Growth is fairly rapid, especially during the first fourteen weeks, during which a pup can gain as much as 3? lbs (1.5 kg) a week. The mother wolf's milk is very nourishing but the cubs benefit from it for only a few months; they are partially weaned at around 20 days (and totally weaned after 5–8 weeks) and then begin to eat food that has been pre-chewed and regurgitated by their mother. When their mobility improves, the pups will beg for food by licking round the mouth of their mother or other pack-members. This stimulates the adults into regurgitating the contents of their stomach. However, like good little carnivorous predators, the pups quickly develop an interest in non-chewed food: from the age of two months they love to gnaw a bone.

Wolf cubs of that age are real little braggarts and already quite strong in comparison to a puppy. Their relationship with their mother is lighthearted and playful. They jump, chase each other, and trample, with

The mother wolf takes care of her little ones, nourishing them by regurgitating morsels of pre-chewed meat on demand. She also cleans their pelage and, by rubbing and licking their stomachs, helps to regulate their intestinal activities.

annoying persistence, on their mother, who submits to these tortures, nips and fur-pulling with grace: her aggressive instincts are totally subdued by the shape and smell of her young.

Relationships between young wolves are very lively and as they grow and their muscular strength increases their energy seems inexhaustible. During play, behavioral scenarios are repeated, and will ultimately be consolidated in adulthood. Their nervous system is subjected to a mul-titude of stimulations that provoke physical and muscu-lar responses, and when they chase each other and jump on the rocks around the den they are not just playing, they are training their nervous systems. How to calculate distances, how much strength to use in jumping, how to keep balance during a difficult crossing, discovering plants or other animals – these are crucial developmen-tal experiences, which they will refine over time, miming and repeating innate and learned behavioral scenarios.

The territory the young wolves explore increases with their physical development; at around six months they are ready to follow their parents in the activities of the hunt. They will learn capture techniques and above all they will get to know the habits and characteristics of their prey.

The "invitation to play", with front legs forward, rear raised, tail wagging and head tossing, is identical to that of domestic dogs. Between young wolves, fighting establishes ranking order and forms personalities. Scrapping, yapping, nipping, and flights, chases and torn ears are the norm among young wolves, especially the males. After their first six months, their physical development and mobility are sufficiently advanced to enable them to begin following their parents or the adults of the pack when they go hunting.

In wolves' lives, a significant amount of information is "culturally" transferred by adults to the young. This ability to learn and to teach has undoubtedly helped wolves to get out of difficult situations and to escape total extinction. For instance, when humans tried to exterminate them by using strychnine, wolves learned to distrust it: they tasted the meat and left it as soon as they suspected it was poisoned. The small dose they absorbed made them slightly ill, but it enabled them to survive. Wolves reach sexual maturity after twenty-two months, when a

new litter has already been born within the pack. It is mostly the females that help look after the new wolf-pups. In this way, they begin to understand the meaning and difficulties of reproduction, an important moment for females of all species. This is often the point at which young wolves disperse from the pack; alternatively, they may stay and attempt to achieve a higher ranking. It seems that, for a wolf, the decision to stay or to go depends on location, individuals and available prey. Mortality remains rather high among young wolves living in areas with high human density. They have to overcome all kinds of real dangers, such as poaching, speeding cars, poisoned bait, and snares, before they acquire the experience necessary for survival.

Conclusion

We hope we have conveyed a message in this book.

We have told you about the wolf, its habits, and its history, but the task of ensuring its safety remains not only in the hands of a few professionals and specialists who work in the field, but also in the hands of the media, who can influence the greatest possible numbers of people. Thanks to the spread of accurate information, the politics of species conservation have begun to have some effect throughout the world, and, little by little, wolves' territories gain ground.

Reintroducing the wolf into the wild is a very complex task with which humans have grappled for only a short time. It seems as if it works. For instance, the reintroduction of wolves in the Yellowstone National Park in 1995 and 1996 is an undeniable success: the first packs are reproducing already. However, wolves don't need much encouragement to regain their lost territories: they are quite capable of recovering them themselves, given time and means. They extend their territory naturally, establishing themselves where they find the ecological conditions most favorable to their needs.

In this respect, the history of the Italian wolf is very significant. The species, which disappeared from the Italian peninsula during the 1970s, has today almost re-conquered the whole of the Alpine chain, as far as the Apennines. This is thanks to major information campaigns such as "Operation St Francis and the wolf," initiated by the World Wildlife Foundation (WWF), and of studies undertaken by experts and volunteers. Another factor is the return of some of the wolf's favorite prey, assisted by reintroduction undertaken during the 1960s.

In France, two wolves were officially recorded in Mercantour National Park, France on November 5 1992; also in November, a wolf was killed near Grenoble. After ninety years of absence, wolves have returned to France.

The park immediately launched an awareness campaign to facilitate this return, but the typical reaction that follows any news of this predator repeated itself here and elsewhere; old fears were revived,

there were debates and polemics, even anti-wolf demonstrations were organized! Fortunately things calmed down and it looks as if the wolf will survive; it has even returned to Switzerland.

To sum up, the wolf "goes it alone." Nature is all-powerful; we think we can tame it; in fact it happens more often that not that we devastate the wilderness, shaping it to suit ourselves, but it takes a very short time for nature to reclaim its rights.

Truly, it is our responsibility, and change must come from deep within us. Our future survival depends on the ecological balance that we are able to develop. It is not enough to ensure the conservation of a species; it requires a worldwide rescue operation. Each action is but a drop of water in the ocean if human behavior towards our planet and its innumerable life-forms is not modified.

The evidence is that we are an ecologically abnormal species: not only do we consume too much, but we consume badly. We need to rediscover the bond that unites us, *Homo sapiens*, with nature; we need to rediscover the harmony of our origins.

For these reasons, nowadays millions of people visit protected regions and take an interest in the lives and destinies of animals like the wolf. They feel the need to restore contact with nature, rediscover equilibrium, and renew themselves in a meadow, on a mountain or in the woods. The fate of our environment and all that it comprises is in our hands. Things can improve or grow worse very quickly. In Norway, the once-increasing wolf population is now in decline because yet again humans have begun hunting them.

So what is our message? Possibly, that we must change our way of life; or that the wolf can teach us ways of living in common and with respect for nature; or even that it is important to get close to the natural world and to internalize it, to become part of it.

It is essential to develop within ourselves a little grain of naturalism, to let it quicken and grow into a meadow, then a wood and finally a forest ... Perhaps it will finish up by being populated – with no more fear – by the wolf!

Recommended Reading

L. Boitani, *Dalla parte del lupo,* Milan : Mondatori, 1982

G. Boscaglia, *Il lupo,* Udine : Lorenzini Editore, 1985

Committee on Management of Wolf and Bear Populations in Alaska, Board on Biology, Commission on Life Sciences, National Research Council, *National Research Council (U.S.). Committee on Management of Wolf and Bear Populations in Alaska. Wolves, bears, and their prey in Alaska : biological and social challenges in wildlife management*, Washington, DC : National Academy Press, 1997.

H. Fischer, *Wolf wars : the remarkable inside story of the restoration of wolves to Yellowstone,* Helena, Mont. : Falcon Press, c1995.

S. J. Gould, *Il pollice del panda,* Rome : Editori Riuniti, 1983

S. A. Johnson & A. Aamodt, *Wolf pack : tracking wolves in the wild,* Minneapolis : Lerner Publications Company, c1985.

K. Lorenz, *And Man Met the Dog,* Milan : Adelphi, 1973

S. Lovari, *Etologia di campagna,* Turin : Boringhieri, 1980

R. Massa, V. Ingegnoli, *Biodiversità estinzione e conservazione,* Turin : UTET, 1999

R. McIntyre, *A society of wolves : national parks and the battle over the wolf,* Rev. ed., Stillwater, MN : Voyageur Press, 1996.

D. Mech, The Wolf, *The Ecology and Behavior of an Endangered Species,* New York : Doubleday, 1970

M. A. Nie, *Beyond wolves : the politics of wolf recovery and management,* Minneapolis : University of Minnesota Press, c2003.

K. R. Jones, *Wolf mountains : a history of wolves along the Great Divide,* Calgary : University of Calgary Press, 2002.

L. M. Stone, *Gray wolves,* Minneapolis : Lerner Publications Co., c2004.

Picture credits

Luigi Accusani/PANDA PHOTO: pp. 73, 126l, 131
Ardeidas/Miguel Angel De La Cruz/PANDA PHOTO: pp. 30–31,
Henry Ausloos/PANDA PHOTO: p. 132b
Alessandro Bardi/PANDA PHOTO: pp. 59, 80–81, 81b, 141t
Maurizio Biancarelli/PANDA PHOTO: pp. 25, 68–69, 96b, 116–117
BIOS/Jean Louis Klein/Marie Luce Hubert/PANDA PHOTO: pp. 3,
22–23, 32, 53, 63, 64–65, 118, 119, 126mr, 128b, 130, 132t, 134–135,
141b
Marco Branchi/PANDA PHOTO: pp. 10b, 19t, 44–45, 97t, 112–113
Marcello Calandrini/PANDA PHOTO: pp. 3, 88–89, 106–107
Giuliano Cappelli/PANDA PHOTO: pp. 21hr, 35, 126ml, 129t, 129m
Ettore Centofanti/NATURA SERVICE: pp. 5, 6, 7, 10t, 11b,12l, 12r,
13b, 16–17, 21br, 24t, 24b, 26r, 27t, 27b, 29, 33, 34, 38l, 38r, 39, 41r,
41l, 47, 48, 52, 54t, 55t, 55bl, 55br, 58, 62, 66, 67, 70t, 70b, 71hl,
71r, 71bl, 84b, 85, 87, 92tl, 92br, 92bl, 100l, 100tr,100bl, 101t, 101b,
104t, 105, 108t, 108m, 108b, 114t, 114b, 115, 122–123, 125, 127l,
127r, 129b, 136r, 137
Giuseppe Corte/PANDA PHOTO: p. 19b
DIA CONTACT/Albert Visage/PANDA PHOTO: p. 17b
Giovanni Fasoli/NATURA SERVICE: pp. 11t, 13t, 136l
FLPA/Terry Whittaker/PANDA PHOTO: pp. 4, 78–79, 104b
Jeff Foot/PANDA PHOTO: pp. 12b, 20t, 20b, 28, 93b
Beata Karp/PANDA PHOTO: pp. 8–9
Gerard Lacz/PANDA PHOTO: pp. 3, 18, 21m, 40–41, 49, 56–57,
60–61, 75, 93t,
Maurizio Lanini/PANDA PHOTO: pp. 50–51, 82–83, 90, 94, 95, 97b,
109, 120–121
LS INTERNATIONAL CARTOGRAPHY, Milan: pp. 21tl, 21bl, 42r,
42l, 43

Giorgio Marcoaldi/PANDA PHOTO: pp. 2, 36–37, 46, 74–75, 76–77,
84t, 86–87, 91, 98–99, 124–125
Kiki Marmori: p. 54b
Marco Melodia/PANDA PHOTO: p. 140
Stefan Meyers/PANDA PHOTO: p. 96t
Franco Pacelli/PANDA PHOTO: pp. 3, 26l, 102–103
Riccardo Polini/PANDA PHOTO: pp. 110–111
Roberto Ragno/PANDA PHOTO: pp. 14–15
Jacqueline and Albert Visage/PANDA PHOTO: pp. 133, 138
Wildlife/Daniel J. Cox/PANDA PHOTO: pp. 72, 126r, 128t, 128m,
139

Front cover: Giorgio Marcoaldi/PANDA PHOTO
Back cover, clockwise from top:
tl: Gerard Lacz/PANDA PHOTO
tr: Marco Branchi/PANDA PHOTO
mr: Marcello Calandrini/PANDA PHOTO
br: Maurizio Biancarelli/PANDA PHOTO
m: Ettore Centofanti/NATURA SERVICE
bl: Maurizio Lanini/PANDA PHOTO
tl: BIOS/Jean Louis Klein/ Marie Luce Hubert/PANDA PHOTO

t: top
b: bottom
l: left
r: right
m: middle

COPYRIGHT © 2004 FOR THE ORIGINAL EDITION
Colophon srl, San Polo 2580, 30125 Venezia
info@colophon.it

Project Editor Andrea Grandese
Editorial Coordinator Rosanna Alberti
Layout Andrea De Porti
Cartography LS International Cartography, Milan

This 2007 edition published by Metro Books,
by arrangement with Colophon srl.

Metro Books
122 Fifth Avenue
New York, NY 10011

ISBN-13: 978-0-7607-8292-7

Printed and bound in Singapore

3   5   7   9   10   8   6   4   2